Matt Miofsky

Fail

what to do when things go wrong

Leader Guide

by Martha Bettis Gee

Abingdon Press / Nashville

Fail
What to Do When Things Go Wrong
Leader Guide

Copyright © 2017 Abingdon Press
All rights reserved.

This book is printed on elemental chlorine-free paper.
ISBN 978-1-5018-4785-1

Scripture quotations unless noted otherwise are taken from the Common English Bible, copyright 2011. Used by permission. All rights reserved.

17 18 19 20 21 22 23 24 25 26 — 10 9 8 7 6 5 4 3 2 1
MANUFACTURED IN THE UNITED STATES OF AMERICA

CONTENTS

TO THE LEADER

Welcome! In this study, you have the opportunity to help a group of learners explore how failure, experienced by all of us at one time or another, can not only be overcome but used as a learning experience to live our lives more fully for God. The study is based on Matt Miofsky's book, *Fail: What to Do When Things Go Wrong.*

Miofsky is lead pastor of The Gathering, a United Methodist Church in St. Louis, Missouri, which was founded with a vision of creating a Christian community that is compelling for new generations. Miofsky believes that many of the greatest lessons in life are learned not when we succeed but when we fall short. People who learn that they can weather even some of the harshest disappointments in life are better prepared for lives of risk-taking boldness and adventure with God. When we learn how to fail, we learn how to live. Using the story of the prophet Jeremiah, Miofsky invites us to explore failure and the lessons that we can learn from it.

Scripture tells us that where two or three are gathered together, we can be assured of the presence of the Holy Spirit working in and through all those gathered. As you prepare to lead, pray for that presence and expect that you will experience it.

The study includes five sessions, and it makes use of the following components:

- the book *Fail: What to Do When Things Go Wrong* by Matt Miofsky;
- the DVD that accompanies the study;
- this Leader Guide.

Participants in the study will also need Bibles, as well as either a spiral-bound notebook for a journal or an electronic means of journaling, such as a tablet. If possible, notify those interested in the study in advance of the first session. Make arrangements for them to get copies of the book so that they can read the introduction and chapter 1 before the first group meeting.

Using This Guide with Your Group

Because no two groups are alike, this guide has been designed to give you flexibility and choices in tailoring the sessions for your group. The session format is listed below. You may choose any or all of the activities, adapting them as you wish to meet the schedule and needs of your particular group.

The leader guide offers a basic session plan designed to be completed in a time frame of about 45 minutes. Besides the basic session plan, you will find additional activities that are optional. You may decide to add these activities or to substitute them for those suggested in the basic plan.

Select ahead of time which activities the group will do, for how long, and in what order. Depending on which activities you select, there may be special preparation needed. The leader is alerted in the session plan when advance preparation is needed.

Session Format

Planning the Session

Session Goals
Scriptural Foundation
Special Preparation

Getting Started

Opening Activity
Opening Prayer

Learning Together

Video Study and Discussion
Book and Bible Study and Discussion
More Activities (Optional)

Wrapping Up

Closing Activity
Closing Prayer

Helpful Hints

Preparing for the Session

- Pray for the leading of the Holy Spirit as you prepare for the study. Pray for discernment for yourself and for each member of the study group.
- Before each session, familiarize yourself with the content. Read the book chapter again.
- Choose the session elements you will use during the group session, including the specific discussion questions you plan to cover. Be prepared, however, to adjust the session as group members interact and as questions arise. Prepare carefully,

but allow space for the Holy Spirit to move in and through the group members and through you as facilitator.

- Prepare the room where the group will meet so that the space will enhance the learning process. Ideally, group members should be seated around a table or in a circle so that all can see each other. Moveable chairs are best because the group will often be forming pairs or small groups for discussion.

- Bring a supply of Bibles for those who forget to bring their own. Also bring writing paper and pens for those participants who do not bring a journal or a tablet or other electronic means of journaling.

- For most sessions you will also need a chalkboard and chalk, a whiteboard and markers, or an easel with large sheets of paper and markers.

Shaping the Learning Environment

- Begin and end on time.
- Create a climate of openness, encouraging group members to participate as they feel comfortable.
- Remember that some people will jump right in with answers and comments, while others will need time to process what is being discussed.
- If you notice that some group members seem never to be able to enter the conversation, ask them if they have thoughts to share. Give everyone a chance to talk, but keep the conversation moving. Moderate to prevent a few individuals from doing all the talking.
- Communicate the importance of group discussions and group exercises.

- If no one answers at first during discussions, do not be afraid of silence. Count silently to ten, then say something such as, "Would anyone like to go first?" If no one responds, venture an answer yourself and ask for comments.
- Model openness as you share with the group. Group members will follow your example. If you limit your sharing to a surface level, others will follow suit.
- Encourage multiple answers or responses before moving on.
- To help continue a discussion and give it greater depth, ask, "Why?" or "Why do you believe that?" or "Can you say more about that?"
- Affirm others' responses with comments such as, "Great" or "Thanks" or "Good insight," especially if it's the first time someone has spoken during the group session.
- Monitor your own contributions. If you are doing most of the talking, back off so that you do not train the group to listen rather than speak.
- Remember that you do not have all the answers. Your job is to keep the discussion going and encourage participation.

Managing the Session

- Honor the time schedule. If a session is running longer than expected, get consensus from the group before continuing beyond the agreed-upon ending time.
- Involve group members in various aspects of the group session, such as saying prayers or reading the Scripture.
- Note that the session guides sometimes call for breaking into smaller groups or pairs. This gives everyone a chance to speak and participate fully. Mix up the groups; don't let the same people pair up for every activity.

- As always in discussions that may involve personal sharing, confidentiality is essential. Group members should never pass along stories that have been shared in the group. Remind the group members at each session: confidentiality is crucial to the success of this study.

1

JEREMIAH'S STORY

Planning the Session

Session Goals

As a result of conversations and activities connected with this session, group members should begin to:

- explore Jeremiah's background and the difficult circumstances he faced;
- examine our own contemporary context;
- acknowledge personal challenges;
- reflect on how we can choose to respond.

Scriptural Foundation

These are the words of Jeremiah, Hilkiah's son, who was one of the priests from Anathoth in the land of

Benjamin. The Lord's word came to Jeremiah in the thirteenth year of Judah's King Josiah, Amon's son, and throughout the rule of Judah's King Jehoiakim, Josiah's son, until the fifth month of the eleventh year of King Zedekiah, Josiah's son, when the people of Jerusalem were taken into exile.

(Jeremiah 1:1-3)

Special Preparation

- Have available a notebook or paper, along with a pen or pencil, for anyone who did not bring a notebook or an electronic device for journaling.
- For the activity "Examine Our Contemporary Context," print the following on a large sheet of paper or a board: The word of the Lord came to the people of (your church name) in the days of _____.
- Then head three separate large sheets of paper or three separate locations on a board with each of the following:
  - o Like Jeremiah, we were all born into a certain location with certain social and historical realities.
  - o Like Jeremiah, we were all born into a particular kind of family.
  - o Like Jeremiah, we all have been thrust into situations that we didn't choose or couldn't control.
- Decide if you will do any of the alternative activities. For the activity in which participants conduct a job interview, you will need a large sheet of paper or a board and marker.
- For the activity of identifying Scriptures, participants will need access to concordances, either the printed variety or an online concordance such as that on BibleGateway.com. You will need sheets of printer or construction paper, tape,

and markers. On a large sheet of paper, in large letters print Jeremiah 1:8:

"Don't be afraid of them,
because I'm with you to rescue you,"
declares the LORD.

Getting Started

Opening Activity

As participants arrive, welcome them to the study. Gather together. If participants are not familiar with one another, provide nametags and make introductions.

Form pairs, and invite partners to discuss the following:

- Where and when in your life, if at all, did you learn how to fail? How did you learn how to deal with failure?

After allowing a few minutes for pairs to discuss, ask one or two volunteers to report some of their conversation to the whole group.

Call the group's attention to Matt Miofsky's idea that some of our best learning experiences actually happen through our setbacks, disappointments, and failures. In this study, participants will explore failure and the lessons that we can learn from it through the lens of Scripture and specifically through the story of the prophet Jeremiah. By encountering how God worked in and through Jeremiah's failures, we will have the opportunity to see how God can also work through our own failures.

Opening Prayer

Pray together, using the following prayer or one of your own choosing:

O Holy God, we are all too aware of our own failures. Yet we have hope that you can use us, as imperfect as we may be. Guide us as we seek to explore more fully how our failures can be a source of growth. Help us trust in your power to shape us according to your purposes. Amen.

Learning Together

Video Study and Discussion

In this series, author and pastor Matt Miofsky introduces us to the prophet Jeremiah. He explores how God worked in and through Jeremiah's failures and setbacks in the hope that we can see how God also can work through our own failures. Session 1 gives us some background about the difficult circumstances in which the prophet lived and to which he was called by God to respond.

- What is grit? What is the relationship between grit and how we respond to difficult circumstances in our lives?
- Miofsky tells us that Jeremiah was born at the worst possible time, in the worst possible place, and given the worst possible job. What about Jeremiah's circumstances would cause us to label them in this way? What message was Jeremiah called to deliver?
- We learn that there is a whole host of circumstances in our own lives that we cannot control. What are some challenging circumstances you have faced, and how have you responded? Would you characterize your own life as risk-taking, bold, adventurous? Why or why not?

Book and Bible Study and Discussion

Explore Jeremiah's Background

Many difficult or challenging circumstances of our lives are largely out of our control. But how we respond to those circumstances will determine whether they build us up or bring us down. It was just such difficult circumstances that Jeremiah was facing.

Ask someone to read aloud the foundational Scripture, Jeremiah 1:1-3. Ask a second volunteer to continue with verses 4-8 and a third to complete the passage by reading verses 9-10. Remind the group that they were just introduced to Jeremiah's historical context in the video segment. Point out that in the era referred to as BC, time is measured in a way that seems backward to us, from the earliest date forward to later ones. So the time period in which Jeremiah was active was from around from 626 BC until at least 587 BC. Discuss:

- The author remarks that Jeremiah was born into a perfect storm. Why does he characterize those times in that way? What was going on?
- Name the three prominent jobs or vocations we can find throughout the Old Testament. Which one does the author identify as the most difficult? Why? What job of the three could Jeremiah have reasonably expected would have been his?
- If you had to write a job description for a prophet, what would you list as skills essential to the position? How would you describe the job responsibilities? How do these responsibilities differ from the conventional wisdom of today's culture about what a prophet did or does?

Examine Our Contemporary Context

Ask someone to read the foundational Scripture aloud again, and point out the contextual "pegs" Jeremiah uses to identify the time period being described. Invite participants to think of particular events in the recent past that might serve as their own contextual pegs; for example, now and in the future, the peg "9/11" would call to mind the attack on the Twin Towers. Or the name "Challenger" might evoke the explosion of the space shuttle, or calling to mind "Pearl Harbor" instantly would evoke the attack on December 7, 1941.

Call the attention of the group to the prompt you posted. ("The word of the Lord came to the people of [your church name] in the days of _____.") Ask:

- How would you complete that open-ended sentence to briefly identify, as Jeremiah does, the larger context in which we live? Other than the year, what identifiers might we use so that people in the future would know what time we are talking about?

Then ask participants to call out, popcorn style, some of the broader cultural, political, social, or geographic realities with which we are presently living. Jot these down on the sheet headed, "Like Jeremiah, we were all born into a certain location with certain social and historical realities." Discuss:

- Which of these realities present significant challenges for us today?

Invite participants to consider the social and historical realities they identified. Discuss:

- We read that Jeremiah lived during a particularly volatile and ultimately tragic period in the history of the Jewish people. How, if at all, would you say that our present context compares with the context in which Jeremiah lived?
- Would you characterize our times as volatile, or would you choose other words to describe them?

Encounter Personal Challenges

Call the group's attention to the second posted statement. ("Like Jeremiah, we were all born into a particular kind of family.") Then ask participants to review what the author says to expand on his statement. And ask them to write in their journals a few sentences describing the family into which each of them was born or adopted.

Point out the third posted statement. ("Like Jeremiah, we all have been thrust into situations that we didn't choose or couldn't control.") Again, ask participants to review what the author says that expands on his statement. Then encourage them to describe in their journals any personal situations or circumstances beyond their control or not of their choosing, either recently or from their past.

After allowing a few minutes for participants to respond in writing, bring the group together for discussion. Acknowledge that some of the responses participants wrote probably reflect deeply personal experiences and realities. Without pressuring anyone to reveal personal information, invite those who are willing to do so to respond to some of the following:

- Many of the personal challenges that participants noted are things that happen *to* us, *around* us, even *within* us—not because of us. Which circumstances in your own life are true of this statement?
- Which are realities for which you bear some responsibility?
- In what ways are you being defined by forces and circumstances outside your direct control? How does it make you feel? Does it make you angry? Defeated or discouraged? Numb? Do you experience some other emotion or a combination of conflicting feelings?

Reflect on How We Might Respond

As the author observes, when we are faced with circumstances and contexts over which we may have little control, we ultimately have two choices. We can choose to focus on our challenges, making them excuses for why things are not working out as we had hoped. Or we can focus on how we are going to respond and how we may follow God even in the midst of those realities. Invite a volunteer to summarize briefly the story that ends the chapter, about the author's good friends who lost their son just a month after his first birthday. Ask:

- How did this couple respond to the tragic circumstances of their baby's death?

Remind the group of the familiar prayer, often called the Serenity Prayer, used by Alcoholics Anonymous and attributed to the theologian Reinhold Niebuhr:

> God, give us grace to accept with serenity the things that cannot be changed,
>
> Courage to change the things which should be changed,
>
> And the Wisdom to distinguish the one from the other.

Ask them to consider the three posted statements about circumstances ("Like Jeremiah...") and to think about what they identified concerning their family of origin, personal challenges, or current political or social contexts. Ask them to choose at least one response that represents a particularly thorny challenge and record in their journals responses to the following:

- In this situation:
  - o What is it that I *cannot* change?
  - o What is it that I *must* change?

Invite them to pray in the coming days for the wisdom to more fully distinguish that which can be changed from that which cannot, as well as to discern more completely what God is calling them to do.

More Activities (Optional)

Research "Be Not Afraid" in the Bible

For Matt Miofsky, Jeremiah 1:8 has served as an inspiration and a source of personal strength in times of hardship. This phrase, or similar affirmations such as "fear not," occurs often in Scripture.

Invite participants to search in a concordance for verses that include these words or similar ones. After allowing a few minutes for research, invite participants to choose relevant verses to print on separate sheets of paper. They may want to emphasize the relevant phrases in some way—for example, the words "Don't be afraid" could be printed with larger letters, in a different font, or in a contrasting color.

Have them tape the completed sheets around the room.

Conduct a Job Interview

Quickly formulate a job description for a prophet, as suggested in the activity "Explore Jeremiah's Background," but do it as a group exercise, not as individuals. Have participants identify skills essential to the position, as well as job responsibilities, and list these on a large sheet of paper.

Invite participants to form pairs. Designate one partner in each pair to be the interviewer (God) and the other to be Jeremiah. Allow a moment for participants to review Jeremiah 1:4-10. Then ask each pair to role-play the interview.

Afterward, review the experience by asking each pair to report briefly on their interview. Ask:

- How did your interview go? What was Jeremiah's response when he heard what the job of prophet entailed?
- If you had been Jeremiah, how do you think you would have responded to God's job offer?
- Have you ever sensed God's call to take on a challenging discipleship task? If so, what was your response? Were you fearful and reluctant? If so, why?

Experience Lamentations

We read that the Book of Lamentations, traditionally attributed to Jeremiah, is a book of laments, or poetic expressions of grief and sadness. While many scholars no longer believe that Jeremiah actually wrote the book, it was likely written around the same time as the Book of Jeremiah.

To experience through poetry what disappointment, sadness, and despair must have felt like in Jeremiah's time, ask participants to read chapter 1 aloud in round-robin fashion—with each participant reading one verse in turn. Following the reading, sit in silence for a few moments. Then invite participants to call out one-word or one-phrase responses that encapsulate for them how the people living through those times must have felt.

Wrapping Up

Invite participants to call out responses, popcorn style, to the following:

- If we don't learn how to fail, there is a danger that we will...
- When we learn how to fail, we...

- What matters is not that we fail, because everyone fails. What counts is that we . . .

Encourage participants to voice any lingering questions and jot these down for further consideration.

Remind the group to read chapter 2 before the next session.

Closing Activity

The author lifts up for us what the author of Ecclesiastes has to say about wisdom and the attributes of a person who has insights into the nature of life. Form two groups to read Ecclesiastes 3:1-8 responsively, beginning by reading verse 1 in unison. ("There's a season for everything and a time for every matter under the heavens. . . .") Then have one group read the first phrase in each verse ("a time for giving birth") and the other group the second phrase ("and a time for dying").

Closing Prayer

Offer the following prayer, which the author uses to close the chapter:

Holy God, sometimes in the midst of circumstances, we fail to respond faithfully to the task that's set before us. So God, give us, through the power of your Holy Spirit, discernment, so that we might let go of the things that we can't control, take hold of the things that we can control, and respond faithfully, believing that you are there to deliver us. We pray these things in Christ's name. Amen.

2

THE DO-OVER

Planning the Session

Session Goals

As a result of conversations and activities connected with this session, group members should begin to:

- explore spiritual idolatry in Jeremiah's time and in ours;
- explore the image of the potter and the clay in Jeremiah;
- examine the idea of God's sovereignty;
- reflect on being molded by God into something beautiful.

Scriptural Foundation

> *Then the LORD's word came to me: House of Israel,*
> *can't I deal with you like this potter, declares the LORD?*

Like clay in the potter's hand, so are you in mine,
house of Israel!

(Jeremiah 18:5-6)

But they said, "What's the use! We will follow our own
plans and act according to our own willful, evil hearts."

(Jeremiah 18:12)

Special Preparation

- Provide journaling materials for those who did not bring them.

- For the activity on the image of the potter and the clay, bring a piece of pottery. Check to see if any participants have experience creating pottery on a wheel. If someone is a potter, ask that person in advance to be prepared to explain how pottery is made. As an alternative, plan to view on YouTube a video segment about pottery making.

- Decide if you will do any of the alternative activities. For the activity on reflecting with clay, get some modeling clay. Check with the leaders of children's classes to see if they have any available to borrow.

- For the do-over game, you will need index cards and pencils or pens.

- Locate either the hymn "Have Thine Own Way, Lord" or "Spirit of the Living God" for the closing activity and arrange for speaking or singing the lyrics. There are a number of versions of each hymn on YouTube.

Getting Started

Opening Activity

As participants arrive, welcome them. If someone is present for this session who did not attend the first session, offer a special welcome.

Gather together. As a way of both reviewing and bringing up to speed those participants who were not present for the first session, do a quick true or false quiz and invite participants to respond, also expanding on their answers to provide some context. Ask:

- True or false: Jeremiah was a reluctant prophet of the Lord.
- True or false: Jeremiah lived in a time when the people of Israel were prospering.
- True or false: Failure is a part of life; the important thing is how we respond to it.

Remind the group that in the previous session, they explored the reality that many things in life are outside their control. In this session, they will explore the opposite idea: that in Jeremiah's time, as in ours, things sometimes go wrong precisely because they are *within* our control—in other words, because of our own decisions, mistakes, or sins.

Opening Prayer

Pray together, using the following prayer or one of your own choosing:

Gracious God, at one time or another all of us have felt powerless in the face of circumstances over which we have no control. Yet we also know that things often go wrong because of our own actions or inactions. By your Spirit, guide us as we seek to recognize and learn from our own mistakes and bad decisions. Amen.

Learning Together

Video Study and Discussion

In session 2, we explore the impact of our bad decisions, mistakes, and sins. We encounter the powerful metaphor of ourselves as misshapen pots, reformed by God as a potter reshapes the clay.

- Life is not as simple as a childhood game, where one can ask for a do-over. Name a time when, had it been possible, you would have asked for a do-over.
- In session 1, the group considered life situations that are beyond our control. What are some circumstances we *can* control?
- Matt Miofsky calls our attention to what he calls the big sin. What is it? Where in your own life can you discern evidence of this sin?
- God directed Jeremiah to pay attention to the potter. What can we learn from how the potter deals with a misshapen pot?

Book and Bible Study and Discussion

Explore Spiritual Idolatry

Remind the group that in book chapter 1, they read that the Book of Jeremiah is not arranged chronologically, and if one reads it from beginning to end the storyline will not be evident. The book also includes poems and speeches along with the narrative. In book chapter 2, we read that the first portion of the book of Scripture up to chapter 20 is almost all oracles of judgment against the sins of Jerusalem. To get a sense of these oracles of judgment, assign one of the following passages to each pair or small group:

- Jeremiah 2:4-13;
- Jeremiah 4:5-8, 19-31;
- Jeremiah 5:1-3; 4-9, 10-17;
- Jeremiah 8:4-17.

After allowing time for each pair or group to read, come together in the large group. Invite a volunteer to read aloud an additional oracle, Jeremiah 6:16-21. Ask group members to respond to the following:

- What feelings did your passage evoke in you? A sense of doom and inevitability, despair, or something else?
- In the additional oracle we just heard, what is meant when God declares the burnt offerings and sacrifices as unacceptable? What do you think might make our worship unacceptable to God?
- How does Miofsky characterize the sins of Jerusalem? What is spiritual idolatry?
- Miofsky observes we can boil down the trouble in our lives to the fact that we replace worship of God with worship of something else. What idols can you identify that seem to have preeminence in our time? Which ones can you name that represent a temptation to you?

Note that Jeremiah's message in these chapters is simple: the people have sinned, and it's too late to avert the punishment that is coming. Invite participants to reflect silently on serious mistakes they have made in their own lives—times when they have deeply hurt other people they love, or when they have acted in ways that are inconsistent with the person they want to be. Invite them to consider the following in silence:

- In what ways has your life been affected by mistakes you have made that you feel cannot be corrected?

- What do you think will be the effect of these mistakes on your future?
- What connection, if any, do you see between some of your mistakes and any idol to which you may have given allegiance—for example, has a preoccupation with acquiring things caused you to divert attention from more important priorities, such as time with family members?

Explore the Image of the Potter and the Clay

Call the group's attention to the piece of pottery you obtained. If you contacted a participant who creates pottery, invite that person to explain something about how he or she practices the craft. Alternatively, view a video segment that you've located about the subject. Invite the group to ask questions, including these:

- How does the potter form a pot on a wheel?
- What happens if the pot gets off center or somehow gets misshapen?

Invite the group to listen as a volunteer reads aloud Jeremiah 18:1-12. Discuss some of the following:

- Up to this point in Jeremiah, the mood has been one of impending doom. What changes in Jeremiah 18? How would you characterize the mood here?
- Miofsky relates a conversation he had with a potter who tells him that, over the course of his career, he has had many more mess-ups than perfect pots. What does this say to you about failure?
- What does the potter tell him about a failed pot?
- When a pot is bad, the potter is able to rebuild something beautiful out of the exact same lump of clay. Do you believe

God can make something beautiful from your failures? Why or why not?

Examine God's Sovereignty

Invite participants to respond to the following:

- How would you define sovereignty? What is God's sovereignty?
- What does the author suggest God is saying in Jeremiah 18:11?
- What does the author have to say about consequences? In your opinion, should consequences be avoided?
- Miofsky observes that, for him, verse 12 is the saddest verse in the Book of Jeremiah. Why? What happened to the people of Judah and to Jeremiah?
- The author notes that some commentators think the words of verse 12 indicate that the people are just being arrogant and stubborn. He disagrees. How does he interpret the words of the verse? What do you think?

Reflect on Being Molded into Something Beautiful

The author invites us to put ourselves in the hands of the Creator, who has the power to turn us into something beautiful. Ask participants to respond silently in their journals to the following:

- Where are the places in my life where I am broken or blemished?
- About what aspects of my life have I resigned myself that they will remain the same—mistakes that cannot be corrected or hurts that cannot be healed?
- Are there people to whom I believe I cannot be reconciled? Are there people who I believe cannot forgive me?
- Are there things in my life that I feel are hopeless?

Encourage participants to return to these questions and their responses in the coming days, offering them up to God for healing and praying that God will make something beautiful from what may seem to be wreckage.

More Activities (Optional)

Reflect with Clay

Give each participant a ball of clay. Invite participants to knead the clay as they reflect on how it feels in their hands. As they work, make the following observations:

1. At first, a ball of clay seems unyielding, hard. But as you work the clay and it becomes warmer, it becomes more pliable, more able to be molded. Ask yourself:
    o   In what ways am I making myself available to God to be molded? What repeated spiritual practices might warm me to God's will for my life?
2. Sculpt the clay into whatever shape or form you choose. It may be a vessel, an animal, or simply a shape that represents something to you. As you work, consider these questions:
    o   What is the shape of my life? In what places does it seem to conform to God's will? Where does it seem to be more resistant?
3. Imagine the situations, circumstances, mistakes, or disappointments that have allowed your life to become misshapen in some way. As you think about them, ask yourself:
    o   What needs to happen in order for my life to conform more nearly to the kind of vessel God would have me be? Does the shape need to be completely broken down so that it can be molded into something beautiful? What are the risks? What might be the blessings?

Invite participants to rework the clay into a shape that is pleasing to them. Close with a time of silence.

Explore the Image of the Broken Earthenware Jug

Invite the group to explore another image of pottery, this time of a broken earthenware jug. Ask participants to read Jeremiah 19 silently. Then ask volunteers to summarize briefly what happens in this chapter—what some have described as street theater, which God directs Jeremiah to perform. Discuss some of the following:

- What is Jeremiah trying to communicate to the people about what is coming?
- Imagine you were one of the people standing at the entry of the Potsherd Gate. Do you think you would find this bit of street theater effective? Why or why not?
- Think about the two metaphors that utilize pottery: the image of a vessel being molded by God, and the image of the earthenware jug being smashed by God. What do these two images communicate to you?

Suggest that the group consider the sign of the broken jug in a slightly different way. Explain that *kintsugi*, the Japanese art of repairing broken pottery using lacquer dusted or mixed with a powdered precious metal such as gold, silver, or platinum, treats breakage and repair as part of the history of an object, rather than something to disguise. Discuss:

- Many of us would consider ourselves to be broken to some degree. What experiences or attitudes can you name that have led to brokenness in you?
- Imagine that God's hand has repaired you, leaving you whole but with the broken places illuminated with the gold from God's hand. In what ways does the story of your brokenness and your redemption by God reveal the story of your life?

How has your history shaped the repaired vessel you have become?

Pray the Do-Over Prayer

Remind the group that at the beginning of the chapter, Miofsky writes about the childhood games he and his friends used to play. A staple of childhood games, he says, is the do-over.

But as Miofsky notes, life is more complicated than that. It is not as simple as a childhood game. Our decisions, our words, our behaviors, our actions, our mistakes, and our failures tend to stick with us for a long time. As adults it is not possible to escape the consequences of our actions by simply requesting a do-over; however, we can identify and reflect on those actions, thus bringing them before God for forgiveness.

Distribute two or more index cards to each participant. Ask them to identify some actions, mistakes, and failures for which they would request a do-over, were such a thing possible. Ask them to list each one on a separate index card, jotting down as many as they wish but without identifying themselves by name. After group members have had time to think and write, collect all the cards.

Invite the group to find a comfortable position for sitting and to settle into silence, breathing out distractions and worries and breathing in a sense of God's presence. Then come together in prayer, bringing before God those things that participants wished they could do over. Read each index card aloud. Then close by offering thanks for God's redeeming power and forgiveness.

Wrapping Up

Ask participants to respond to the following:

- When I feel that it's no use, my hope is in…
- When I think nothing can turn this thing around, I look for redemption from…

- When I am sure my life is defined by my past, I look to the future in...

The author reminds us what happened to the people of Judah: they refused to turn again to their God. The people rejected God's invitation. The Babylonians came, and many of the people were killed. Many others were exiled, carried off to Babylon. Some of them fled. Jeremiah was kidnapped and taken to Egypt. Scripture tells us that the deserted land became desolate and the temple was destroyed.

Eventually, the people returned. Encourage participants to reflect on the open-ended statements they just considered, knowing that in spite of past failures and difficult consequences, God is in charge and, through Jesus Christ, will redeem us.

Remind participants to read book chapter 3 before the next session.

Closing Activity

Sing a Hymn

Sing or recite together the hymn you chose—either "Have Thine Own Way, Lord" or "Spirit of the Living God."

Closing Prayer

Offer the following prayer, which is part of the prayer given by the author at the end of the chapter 2:

God, we thank you that even in a difficult story like Jeremiah's, with lots of sin, lots of messing up, and lots of judgment, there is also hope. We are grateful that it is never too late, that you are a God who has power in our lives and can do beautiful things with messed-up people like us. In Jesus, forgive us, reshape us, and mold us into something beautiful. Amen.

3

IN THE PIT

Planning the Session

Session Goals

As a result of conversations and activities connected with this session, group members should begin to:

- explore a low point in Jeremiah's life;
- examine two elements of lament as revealed in a lament of Jeremiah;
- encounter redemption from an unlikely source;
- reflect on responding to life's low points.

Scriptural Foundation

So they seized Jeremiah, threw him into the cistern of the royal prince Malchiah, within the prison quarters,

and lowered him down by ropes. Now there wasn't any
water in the cistern, only mud, and Jeremiah began to
sink into the mud.

(Jeremiah 38:6)

LORD, *you enticed me, and I was taken in.*
You were too strong for me, and you prevailed.
Now I'm laughed at all the time;
everyone mocks me.

(Jeremiah 20:7)

Sing to the LORD,
praise the LORD,
for he has rescued the needy
from the clutches of evildoers.
(Jeremiah 20:13)

Special Preparation

- Provide materials for journaling for anyone who did not bring them.
- For the activity about responding to life's low points, print the following prompts on a large sheet of paper or a board:
  o At my lowest point, I was angry with God about...
  o I was (was not) able to be honest with God in my feelings about...
  o At my lowest point, I found hope in...
  o I was able to move forward because of...
- Decide if you will do any of the alternative activities. For the plaque, you will need sheets of cardstock or posterboard cut into pieces approximately 9-by-12 inches, plus pencils, colored markers, and scratch paper.
- For the activity about laments, participants will need access to smartphones or to Wi-Fi for their tablets.

- For the fishbowl activity, recruit three volunteers in advance. Ask one to be prepared to play the part of King Zedekiah, one Ebed-melech, and one Jeremiah. Refer all three volunteers to today's Scripture in Jeremiah 38, as well as Jeremiah 37 and the material in book chapter 3. Plan to set up four chairs in a circle in the center of your space.

Getting Started

Opening Activity

As participants arrive, welcome them to the study.

Gather together. Call the group's attention to the story that opens this chapter, about what happened to John and Jennifer and the low point they experienced. Invite participants to form pairs and discuss the following:

- When did you experience a low point—a time when the wind was taken out of your sails and you felt as if you would sink?

Ask for a show of hands for the following:

- Was your low point completely fixable, something that could be solved?
- Or was it truly a tragic happening, something that was beyond fixing and that had a devastating impact on your life?

Invite the group to discuss:

- Regardless of whether your low point was life-changing and tragic, how did you feel? Were you overwhelmed? Discouraged? How did you respond to those feelings?

Tell participants that in this session, they will be introduced to a significant low point in Jeremiah's life.

Opening Prayer

Pray together, using the following prayer or one of your own choosing:

Loving God, we know you have promised to be with us, both in our times of joy and in our times of deepest sorrow and despair. As we explore your word today, give us eyes to see and ears to hear the insights we can gain as together we seek to discern your will for our lives. Amen.

Learning Together

Video Study and Discussion

In session 3, we explore a low point in Jeremiah's life—when he was thrown into a cistern where he was in danger of dying a slow death. We discover that his redemption from this dire situation came from an unexpected quarter. In examining a passage that reflects Jeremiah's response to this experience, we explore the contradictory elements of honest anger and hope for the future that are both inherent in a lament.

- When Jeremiah was thrown into the cistern, he had hit rock bottom—both literally and figuratively. In your own life, can you identify a time when you hit rock bottom? Did you have the experience of wondering whether it was even worth it to take the next step? What did you do? How were you released from the pit?
- What does Matt Miofsky identify as the two essential elements of a lament such as Jeremiah's?
- He notes that if we ever let go of either essential element, we are in danger of being in deep trouble. What are the risks in letting go of each one?

Book and Bible Study and Discussion

Explore a Low Point in Jeremiah's Life

Invite volunteers to retell quickly the story of Jeremiah's vision from God calling him to visit the potter's house. Ask someone to read aloud once again Jeremiah 18:12. Ask:

- Why does the author suggest that this passage is a turning point in Jeremiah's story? What happened?

Ask the group to read silently Jeremiah 38:2-6 and to recall the information in book chapter 3 about the passage. Then discuss some of the following:

- What two realities does the author identify in this passage?
- He notes that there is an interesting difference between being negative and being truthful. How would you describe the difference? Has there ever been a time when you tried to be truthful about a situation and were accused of being negative? How did you deal with the situation?
- The author takes issue with the idea that lowering Jeremiah into the cistern was more merciful than killing him outright. Why? How do you respond?

Examine Jeremiah's Lament

Point out that in session 1, the group read Lamentations 1 in order to connect with the feelings of despair and grief that the exiles must have experienced. Miofsky invites us to examine a lament of Jeremiah's found in Jeremiah 20.

Remind the group that the Book of Jeremiah is not arranged chronologically, and tell them that a volunteer will read verses 7-12. Then the whole group will read verse 13 in unison. Following that, a second volunteer will complete the passage by reading verses 14-18 aloud. Ask the group to listen carefully as the passage is read. Discuss some of the following:

- What did you notice about what was communicated in verse 13, as opposed to the verses you heard before that verse and immediately after it?
- What is the double truth that laments hold together?
- The author observes that we can get ourselves into deep trouble when we are at low points in our lives if we ever let go of either element of lamentation. What is the danger in letting go of hope? of honest anger?
- He suggests that the worst approach a person can take is to be unable to be angry toward God. Why? Do you agree or disagree with this contention? How do you respond to God when you are faced with what may seem to be insurmountable difficulties?

Invite someone to summarize the story the author relates of the pastor going through a difficult divorce. Note that, though the pastor acknowledged he was angry and felt that Jesus was not at that time doing anything for him, he was still able to hold onto his faith. Discuss:

- In difficult situations, how, if at all, have you been able to balance honest anger with a sense of hope? Where do you find acceptance for your raw feelings? What are sources of hope for you?

Encounter Redemption from an Unlikely Source

Ask a volunteer to read aloud Jeremiah 38:7-13. Discuss:

- Jeremiah's rescuer's name is mentioned specifically several times in this passage. Why is this significant?

38

- Think about times when you have been at low points in your life. When, if at all, has help come from an unexpected place or in the form of an unlikely person?
- Can you name a time when you have been able to hear someone's anger? When have you been a source of hope for someone else? How do you respond to a person whom you know to be going through a difficult time?

Reflect on Responding to Life's Low Points

Revisit with the group the opening activity in which they identified low points in their lives, whether they were things relatively fixable or true crises or tragedies. Suggest that now participants reflect silently about the single lowest point each can remember in his or her life, a time when he or she may not have been able to see a way forward. Perhaps it was an event or situation sometime in the past, or he or she could be experiencing such a time right now. Ask them to take a few moments to respond in their journals to the posted prompts:

- At my lowest point, I was angry with God about...
- I was (was not) able to be honest with God in my feelings about...
- At my lowest point, I found hope in...
- I was able to move forward because of...

More Activities (Optional)

Create a Reminder Plaque

Recall that in book chapter 1, Miofsky discloses to us that Jeremiah 1:8 is a source of inspiration for him, a verse he turns to for personal strength during hardship. "Don't be afraid" is a constant message threading its way through Scripture.

Distribute scratch paper. Ask participants to identify one or more circumstances in their present lives about which they have anxiety or fear. On the scratch paper, ask them to jot down words or phrases that identify for them their emotions about the situation or particular details that are worrisome.

When they have had time to identify words and phrases, give each person a piece of card stock or prepared posterboard. Provide colored markers. In the center of the sheet, have them print the words, "Don't be afraid." Using smaller letters, have them print around the central message the words and phrases they jotted down. They can arrange them in any way they choose. Encourage them to post their completed plaques in places where they can see them regularly, such as on their refrigerators or near bathroom mirrors.

Research and Write Laments

Invite participants to review what the author has to say about laments; then invite them to do some further online research about laments. They might also read through the Book of Lamentations and some of the communal and individual psalms of lament in the Book of Psalms, such as Psalm 38 or Psalm 137.

Remind them of what the author has to say about the two elements that are key to laments: honest anger at God and a sense of hope. Then invite them to try their hands at writing laments. It might be an individual lament about a personal low point someone has experienced in the past or is experiencing now, or it could be a communal lament about a situation or circumstance that is affecting the community, the nation, or the world.

After allowing time for participants to reflect and write, invite volunteers to read aloud their laments. Encourage participants who enjoy writing to try writing laments as a part of their devotional time.

Engage in a Fishbowl Drama

Invite the three volunteers each to take a seat in the circle of chairs (see Special Preparation earlier in this session). Identify each of the three characters for the group, or ask the volunteers to identify themselves. The group will hear from all three, each character describing the situation in Jeremiah 38 from his own perspective.

At any point in the conversation, anyone else in the group can take the empty chair and join the conversation, asking questions or challenging statements. They can also take the parts of Shephatiah, Gedaliah, Jucal, or Pashhur, the men in Jeremiah 38 who reported Jeremiah's words to the people.

Begin with King Zedekiah, then move to Ebed-melech and finally to Jeremiah, with each describing what happened, how he was feeling, and why he acted as he did. When the conversation has run its course, debrief the experience. If these questions have not already been addressed, discuss the following:

- What motivated King Zedekiah to act as he did? What do you think he was afraid of?
- What might have motivated Ebed-melech to intercede on Jeremiah's behalf?
- Imagine how Jeremiah must have felt as he struggled all alone to survive in the cistern. What might he have been thinking and feeling?

Wrapping Up

The author invites us to hold onto two thoughts: that in our lowest points, we need to be honest about our anger but hold onto our hope; and we should remember that our lowest point will not be our last point. Encourage the group to continue reflecting on the following in the coming days:

- As I look back on low points from my past, what wisdom and lessons, if any, have I learned?

- What parts of those experiences might have the power to shape the rest of my life?

Remind participants to read book chapter 4 before the next session.

Closing Activity

Invite the group to experience the lament in Jeremiah 20 in a slightly different way. Have them read the passage in round-robin fashion, with each person reading one verse until the entire passage is read. But instead of reading verse 13 where it falls, ask the group to say it aloud following each of the other verses, as a reminder that at our low points, faithful hope endures in the midst of our honest anger.

All (after each verse):

> *Sing to the* Lord,
>> *praise the* Lord,
>>> *for he has rescued the needy*
>>> *from the clutches of evildoers.*

Closing Prayer

Offer the following prayer, which is part of the prayer given by the author at the end of chapter 3:

God, we thank you that you are a God big enough to hear our anger. But God, we also pray that you'd give us the knowledge to hold onto your hope, a hope that declares that our low points are not our last points, and that there is life on the other side of the pit. May we use the lessons that we learn in our low points to walk with others through the low points in their lives. We pray these things in Christ's name. Amen.

4

FINDING HOPE

Planning the Session

Session Goals

As a result of conversations and activities connected with this session, group members should begin to:

- explore Jeremiah's unlikely purchase;
- experience a prayer of trustful incredulity;
- encounter the nature of hope;
- reflect on investing in hope.

Scriptural Foundation

> "The LORD of heavenly forces, the God of Israel, proclaims:
> Take these documents—this sealed deed of purchase
> along with the unsealed one—and put them into a clay
> container so they will last a long time. The LORD of

heavenly forces, the God of Israel, proclaims: Houses,
fields, and vineyards will again be bought in this land."

(Jeremiah 32:14-15)

You have been saying, "This city will be handed over to
the king of Babylon through sword, famine, and disease."
But this is what the LORD, the God of Israel, says: I will
gather them from all the countries where I have scattered
them in my fierce anger and rage. I will bring them back
to this place to live securely. They will be my people, and I
will be their God.

(Jeremiah 32:36-38)

Special Preparation

- Provide journaling materials for those who did not bring them.
- As a review of the previous session, print and post the following words and phrases on a large sheet of paper or a board: sword, famine, or disease; King Zedekiah; cistern; mud; Ebed-melech; thirty men; old rags and scraps of clothing; ropes.
- If possible in advance, recruit a participant whom you know to be a strong and expressive reader to read aloud Jeremiah's prayer in Jeremiah 32:17-25.
- For the closing activity, locate the song "You Are Mine" by David Haas, to be sung or read. Arrange for accompaniment as needed. One version can be found on YouTube.

Getting Started

Opening Activity

As participants arrive, welcome them to the study.

Gather together. With a show of hands, ask who among the participants dabbles in the stock market. Then ask:

- How do you decide when and in what stocks to invest?

Then ask:

- How do you make a decision about a business opportunity that may present risks, such as a large purchase you are planning to make sometime in the future that suddenly presents itself as possible now, but which may stretch your budget beyond its capacity?

Point out that as book chapter 4 opens, Matt Miofsky relates a piece of advice Warren Buffet offers about investing. Invite a volunteer to describe that advice. Then tell the group that in this session, participants will explore an insight from Scripture: that it is in the midst of our greatest setbacks, tragedies, and disappointments where we may encounter our greatest opportunities.

Opening Prayer

Pray together, using the following prayer or one of your own choosing:

Eternal God, we give thanks that in our darkest times, you are there. Guide us as we seek to discern the possibilities and opportunities that may be presenting themselves, even in the midst of the setbacks and disappointments we all experience. Amen.

Learning Together

Video Study and Discussion

In session 4, we encounter a puzzling story of an unlikely investment. With the Babylonians literally outside the gates of Jerusalem, Jeremiah exercises his familial right to purchase a field from his cousin Hanamel—and at what, in more normal times, would have been fair market value! We encounter what the author refers to as Jeremiah's prayer of trustful incredulity. And we consider the nature of hope and what might be called investing in hope even in the face of what may seem to be a hopeless situation, when disaster looms.

- It is often when we have the greatest setbacks or disappointments that we find the greatest opportunities. When, if at all, has this been your experience?
- Have you ever prayed what Miofsky labels a prayer of trustful incredulity? What were the circumstances? What happened?
- We acknowledge that we should not expect to avoid the consequences of actions we take. Think of a time when you were about to undergo consequences as the result of a mistake. With the Babylonians at your gates, how did you respond? With despair, with hope for a different perspective in the future, or with some other emotion?

Book and Bible Study and Discussion

Explore Jeremiah's Unlikely Purchase

Do a quick review of the story from the previous session by inviting participants to refer to Jeremiah 38:2-13 and give the significance of each of the names and words you posted before the session.

Set the context for the Scripture by reading aloud Jeremiah 32:1 and summarizing for the group some of the background information the author gives us. Then invite participants to listen as two volunteers take the parts of Zedekiah and Jeremiah, with one reading Jeremiah 32:2-5 and the other reading verses 6-15. Encourage them to review quickly what the author has to say about this passage. Then discuss some of the following:

- Recall Warren Buffett's investing advice. Would you say Jeremiah's purchase of the field is an example of buying when everyone else is selling?
- The author observes that, at the precise moment when Jeremiah and his prophecies are being vindicated, God decides to make a statement of hope. Why?
- What is the source of the hope Jeremiah is demonstrating? Is it hope that disaster would be averted? Is it hope that at some time in the future, normal life will be restored? Is it something else?

Experience a Prayer of Trustful Incredulity

Invite the group to listen as the volunteer you recruited reads Jeremiah's prayer in Jeremiah 32:17-25. Discuss the following:

- Miofsky tells us that one scholar calls this a prayer of trustful incredulity. Have you ever uttered such a prayer—one that expresses trust in God despite having at best some reservations or even outright disbelief? What were the circumstances?

Ask someone now to read verses 26-27. Discuss:

- We might paraphrase God's response to Jeremiah in this way: "Now that I have you at this lowest point, do you trust in my power? Do you trust that I can do something through you?" In looking back on some of your lowest points, how do you think you would have responded to God in those situations when asked those questions?
- Miofsky quotes science fiction writer Ray Bradbury, who said, "Remember that we are an impossibility in an impossible universe." What is meant by this statement? How

does the author interpret it in the light of God's ability to make things new?

Point out that the hope Jeremiah was called by God to communicate did not mitigate the consequences the people were to suffer. Recall that it's oftentimes at the point of our greatest doubt, when we are most questioning God, that God finds the greatest possibilities in our life. Ask:

- What has been your experience of possibilities emerging from low points in your life? Whether or not you have experienced this, do you think it is sometimes the case? Can you think of examples?
- During low points, what spiritual practices and tools of the faith might help you discern possibilities that you might otherwise miss?

Encounter the Nature of Hope

For the remainder of Jeremiah 32, God first reminds Jeremiah of the judgment that is coming then promises the people that, after suffering the consequences of their actions, they will be restored to the land. Refer the group again to verses 36-37. Discuss some of the following:

- What do you think is meant by the phrase "Remember the future"?
- In recalling Warren Buffett's admonition about investing, Miofsky invites us to invest in hope. What do you think the author means?
- The author points out that hope is not a feeling; rather, hope is a choice that God asks us to make. When, if ever, have you experienced hope as a choice in your life?

Reflect on Investing in Hope

Ask the group to consider ways in which members of the faith community might make a difference for themselves or for others going through very dark times. Encourage participants to think about the following questions then write their thoughts and responses in their journals.

- How might I and others in the faith community invest in hope on behalf of another person? What words and actions might be helpful? What platitudes or inactions might serve to be detrimental?

More Activities (Optional)

Put Yourself in the Text

Ask a volunteer to read aloud Jeremiah 32:1-3a. Suggest that group members close their eyes and imagine that they are living in Jerusalem during the time of Jeremiah. Say the following:

> You are living in Jerusalem, and the situation is dire. The Babylonian army is outside the gates, besieging the city. Because of the siege, there is no more food in the city. You and your family are starving, and there is no end in sight. Jerusalem has strong walls, so its residents can hold off for a while. But the Babylonian army is waiting, and it is inevitable that the city will fall. And when it does, the Babylonians will sack the city. You know there is a strong possibility that you and your family will be carried off into exile, if indeed you survive. What Jeremiah has been prophesying for years is imminent.

As they imagine themselves in this situation, invite participants to call out responses to the following:

- What are your emotions as you face what is to come?
- What are your biggest fears? Your most pressing uncertainties?

Continue imagining the following:

> You have just heard a perplexing rumor. Apparently in the midst of all that has happened, Jeremiah the prophet has purchased the field of Anathoth from his cousin Hanamel, son of his uncle Shallum. And not for an insignificant price either; Jeremiah has paid a substantial sum—seventeen shekels of silver! All for a piece of land, admittedly family land, that will be rendered worthless when the Babylonians take over.
>
> You hurry down to the court of the guard to see if this ridiculous rumor is true. And sure enough, there is Jeremiah with the sealed deed of purchase, in the presence of his cousin and of those who witnessed the signing. And now you can hear Jeremiah speaking to Baruch the scribe. You move closer so you can hear what he is saying: "...the LORD of heavenly forces, the God of Israel, proclaims: Houses, fields, and vineyards will again be bought in this land" [Jeremiah 32:15].

Invite participants to call out responses to the following:

- What are your emotions on hearing that Jeremiah has purchased the field? How do you respond to what he has done?

- Upon hearing his declaration that houses, fields, and vineyards will again be bought in this land, do you experience a sense of hope? Why or why not? Do you find Jeremiah's declaration to be trustworthy or not?

Invest in Hope by Walking Alongside

Investing in hope during our darkest time means living now like we believe that something different is coming. Discuss the following:

- We all experience low points in our lives, some more than others. But what about people who are living in absolute poverty or with debilitating conditions for which there literally is no hope of survival or under conditions of modern slavery or in conflict zones? Invite the group to think about what would constitute investing in hope for these people.
- For people whose lives are about continually walking through the valley of the shadow of death, what is our responsibility as Christians to them? How do we walk alongside these people, investing in hope on their behalf?

Encourage participants to brainstorm concrete ways the group might choose to act in hope for those whose lives may seem hopeless. How can we guide resources in the direction of people made vulnerable by the conditions of their lives? How can we advocate for more humane and just systems in which hope becomes a choice for all?

Wrapping Up

Invite someone to summarize briefly the story with which Miofsky ends the chapter, about his pastor friend whose call was to a church in East St. Louis. This friend, on being asked why he thought his church was surviving and thriving, responded that his congregants really believe that God has a future for them and that their best days are ahead.

In light of the congregants' inspiring attitude, invite participants to respond, popcorn style, to the following:

- When I think about low points in my life, I feel…
- I believe God really will see me through the disappointments and tragedies I may face because…

Remind the group to read book chapter 5, the final chapter, before the next session.

Closing Activity

The author encourages us to live now as if we believe those words that God spoke to Jeremiah at the beginning of the book of Scripture:

> *"Don't be afraid of them,*
> *because I'm with you to rescue you,"*
> *declares the LORD.*
> *(Jeremiah 1:8)*

Sing or recite together the song "You Are Mine."

Closing Prayer

Offer the following prayer, which is part of the prayer given by the author at the end of chapter 4:

Gracious and holy God, we pray for those of us who struggle to believe that you have something good planned for us, that you can actually forgive us, that the broken things in our lives can be fixed, that something better is around the corner. Help us to hope, to start living now with the joy and confidence and assurance that you have more of a story to write in our lives. We pray in the mighty name of the resurrected Christ. Amen.

5

ON THE OTHER SIDE OF EXILE

Planning the Session

Session Goals

As a result of conversations and activities connected with this session, group members should begin to:

- explore Jeremiah's letter to the exiles;
- explore the metaphorical, spiritual event of exile;
- examine two lies of false prophets;
- reflect in their own lives on a future with hope.

Scriptural Foundation

> *The LORD of heavenly forces, the God of Israel,*
> *proclaims to all the exiles I have carried off from*

Jerusalem to Babylon: Build houses and settle down;
cultivate gardens and eat what they produce. Get
married and have children; then help your sons find
wives and your daughters find husbands in order that
they too may have children. Increase in number there so
that you don't dwindle away. Promote the welfare of the
city where I have sent you into exile. Pray to the LORD
for it, because your future depends on its welfare.
(Jeremiah 29:4-7)

I know the plans I have in mind for you, declares the
Lord; they are plans for peace, not disaster, to give you
a future filled with hope. When you call me and come
and pray to me, I will listen to you. When you search
for me, yes, search for me with all your heart, you will
find me.
(Jeremiah 29:11-13)

Special Preparation

- Provide journaling materials for those who do not bring any.
- For the opening activity, post on a large sheet of paper or board the following quotation from J. R. R. Tolkien in *The Return of the King*: "Oft hope is born when all is forlorn." Below that quotation, print the following phrases:
  o   a difficult call
  o   in the potter's house
  o   thrown in the cistern
  o   the unlikely purchase of a field
- On two separate large sheets of paper or two locations on a board, print the following:
  o   Lie 1: It is okay to engage in self-destructive behavior when I am in a place of exile.

54

- o Lie 2: Because I'm a loser, I can't expect much better than what I am experiencing in my place of exile.
- For the closing activity, either print the litany on a large sheet of paper, or make copies for participants from this leader guide.
- Decide if you will do either of the alternative activities. For the activity of imagining places of exile, list the following phrases on a large sheet of paper or a board:
  - o A Syrian refugee family in a refugee camp
  - o An immigrant awaiting news on green card status
  - o A woman in a domestic violence shelter
  - o A worker trapped in a dead-end job
  - o A student who has just been rejected from her three top college choices

Getting Started

Opening Activity

As participants arrive, welcome them to this final session of the study.

Gather together. Call attention to the quotation and phrases that you posted before the session. Invite participants to quickly review the story of Jeremiah by glancing over the chapter titles in the study book.

Ask someone to read aloud the posted quotation from J. R. R. Tolkien. Matt Miofsky observes that Tolkien's statement is certainly true of Jeremiah's story. In fact, most of what we read in Jeremiah presents some harsh realities. Yet at the end, when the Babylonian army takes the city and the people are carried into exile, the Book of Jeremiah has some of the most hopeful messages in all of Scripture. In this session participants will encounter those hopeful messages and reflect on their meanings.

Opening Prayer

Pray together, using the following prayer or one of your own choosing:

Loving God, sometimes we feel discouraged or despondent about the circumstances of our lives. We feel helpless in the face of the loss of jobs and income, over a divorce or the death of a loved one, over estrangement from a friend. Sometimes we are in despair about our own bad decisions and their consequences. We—and indeed our world—can use some good news! Guide us as we encounter your message of hope, so that we may make it our own. Amen.

Learning Together

Video Study and Discussion

In this final session we are introduced to a letter from Jeremiah to the exiles. We encounter here some hopeful messages, and we discover that some of the most hopeful messages in all of Scripture are threaded throughout the Book of Jeremiah. We have the opportunity to reflect on their meanings both for the exiles in Jeremiah's time and for us in our own places of exile.

- Exile, we discover, is about disrupting a person's sense of identity. How, if at all, have you experienced exile? In what ways did a sense of exile threaten your understanding of who you are?
- When have you allowed a difficult circumstance or situation to stop you from living your life, either by putting off making an important life decision or by not fully engaging in the routine experiences of living?
- What are the two lies Miofsky identifies that we may hear from false prophets when we are at low points in our lives?

What do you think makes us more vulnerable to those lies? What distortions about ourselves are we meant to accept if we embrace those lies?

Book and Bible Study and Discussion

Explore a Letter to the Exiles

To set the stage for hearing Jeremiah's letter, ask someone to read Jeremiah 29:1-2. Note that in ancient times, letters were not just written documents. Rather they were read out loud and interpreted to the recipients by messengers.* With this in mind, invite participants to imagine they are exiles gathered to hear the letter from Jeremiah read. Ask a volunteer to read verses 4-14 aloud. Discuss:

- Jeremiah wrote this letter to those who had been carried off in exile when Jeremiah was still residing in Jerusalem. This letter comes to the exiles after they have experienced many years of hearing Jeremiah prophesying and delivering messages about the coming doom. As an exile, how do you think you would have felt when hearing these words read by a messenger?
- Miofsky tells us that the letter is not the chronological end of the story, but it is the thematic end. What do you think he means by that?

Explore the Metaphorical, Spiritual Event of Exile

Ask group members to review quickly what Miofsky has to say about exile as a war strategy used by the Babylonians. Discuss the following:

- There are two major events in Israel's history that shaped the people's imagination. More than just historical events, these

---

* *Jeremiah*, by R. E. Clements. In *Interpretation: A Bible Commentary for Teaching and Preaching*, James L. May, Series Editor (Atlanta: John Knox Press, 1988), p. 171.

two are metaphorical, spiritual events that have happened to all of us. What are they?

- What are the characteristics of exile that are identified by the author?

Discuss ways in which the experience of exile applies to our own lives:

- Have you ever felt you were in a place of exile, where you were distanced from where you wanted to be and didn't know how to get back? Have you been in a place of waiting for things to change that you can't control? If so, describe how you felt during those times.
- Miofsky states that exile is all about disrupting one's identity. Why, and in what ways?
- What is Jeremiah's first piece of advice to the exiles? How would you have reacted to it?
- Respond to Miofsky's question: Have you ever allowed the circumstances of your life to stop you from living, to stall you from life? If so, what were the circumstances, and in what ways did you put a hold on your life?

Examine Two Lies of False Prophets

Invite someone to reread aloud Jeremiah 29:8. Ask participants to describe what was happening that caused Jeremiah to give this caution to the exiles. Then call their attention to the two lies that you posted before the session, to which we are vulnerable in situations of exile. Miofsky tells us that the first lie is intended to take us down and the second lie is intended to keep us down.

Form two groups. Give each group a sheet or board with one of the lies posted on it. Invite participants in each group to identify one example of an exile experience that people often encounter. It might be a divorce, a job loss, a disastrous financial loss, or some other experience that might plunge a person into a place of exile. Ask them to discuss how their assigned lie might manifest itself in that exile experience. Have each group choose a scribe to make notes on the sheet of paper or board.

After allowing time for the two groups to discuss, have each group bring the sheet or board back to the large group and report, sharing some of the conversation from their group and any questions that surfaced. If the following questions do not emerge in the discussion, pose them for discussion now:

- Miofsky observes that when a person is in a place of exile, God sees that there's an endpoint that individual can't see. How do you respond to that?
- What do you think it means that, even if we cannot see a good end to a situation, God is in control? Do you think it means God will step in at every low point we experience, regardless of whether we hold responsibility for it or not? Is there a difference between God's action to determine a situation and ways in which God is working in the midst of and through a situation?

Reflect on a Future with Hope

Call the group's attention to one of the foundational Scriptures, Jeremiah 29:11-13, and have someone read it aloud again. Then invite participants to reflect on the following by writing in their journals:

- At this moment, where do you find yourself? Do you doubt whether the future has anything in store for you? Are you wondering if what you're experiencing now is all there is? Or are you presently in a place of happiness, or of complacency? Regardless of where you find yourself, identify whether you generally are hopeful about the future or are instead experiencing a sense of hopelessness. What comfort, if any, is the knowledge that God takes the long view?

- The passage reassures us that God is always working for our welfare and not for our harm. What is your sense of the role God is playing in your life at present?

Encourage participants to return to their reflections on these questions in the coming days. Regardless of whether they currently are in places of exile at present or are feeling they are about to enter the Promised Land, suggest that they use the foundational Scriptures for this session as a part of their devotional time in the coming days.

More Activities (Optional)

Practice Prayers for Our Enemies

Invite a volunteer to read aloud Jeremiah 29:7. Note that in the passage, the Lord tells the people, in the midst of the circumstances when life didn't work out the way they had planned, not just to invest in hope but also to pray for the people who had captured them. Discuss:

- Do you agree that praying for our enemies is a difficult spiritual exercise? What are some occasions when you have succeeded or failed to do this?
- What are some signs that you are turning a corner in a relationship with someone who has hurt you?

One way of taking back power in a situation where you feel powerless is to pray for the things that you want to see changed. Suggest that participants engage in an exercise of intercessory prayer. Ask them to identify things they long to see resolved or changed. It could be personal low points that they are presently experiencing, such as divorces or job losses, or it could be concerns they have for the nation or world. If someone has wronged the participant as a part of his or her personal low point, the participant should consider whether the prayer might involve asking God for the strength to forgive.

Invite participants to find comfortable positions for sitting and then to close their eyes and breathe in and out deeply several times, centering themselves. After a few moments, ask them to cup their hands in front of them, imagining the various aspects of the low points or exile experiences that they yearn to change. If there are people toward whom they would like to make a change of attitude or actions, invite them to visualize those people as well. Suggest that they imagine holding those circumstances or people in their cupped hands and extending their hands to lift them up before God.

Ask participants to offer prayers to God on behalf of those people or circumstances. If they are unable to articulate their feelings, encourage them to offer the person or situation up to God wordlessly, trusting that God will frame their prayers according to God's purposes. After a time of silence, close with "Amen."

Imagine Places of Exile

Call the group's attention to the list that you posted at the beginning of the session of people experiencing exile. Invite participants if they wish to add more categories of exiled people. Ask them to imagine being one of the people on the list and to write a brief paragraph in each of their journals describing the following:

- The details of the situation in which the person finds him- or herself
- Aspects of the situation that are the most worrisome
- What seems transitory
- What seems hopeless
- In what or whom hope might be found

After allowing time for participants to write, invite one or two volunteers to read what they wrote.

Wrapping Up

Remind the group that, ten years after the events described in this session, the Babylonians finally came, destroying the temple and taking the city. Invite volunteers to summarize briefly what became of Jeremiah and how, years later, God fulfilled the promise to return the people.

Miofsky makes the connection between Jeremiah's messages of hope and the teachings and person of Jesus Christ, the leader God raised up. He observes that we have a God who not only promises to love us and give us a future with hope but who has actually done just that in sending his son, Jesus Christ.

Ask participants to respond, popcorn style, to the following words or phrases:

- the hope in dealing with failure
- the hope of being molded by God
- balancing anger with hope
- investing in hope
- a future with hope

Closing Activity

Wrap up the study by forming two groups and inviting participants to join in reciting a litany based on a quotation from the book *A Door Set Open: Grounding Change in Mission and Hope* by Peter L. Steinke (Herndon, VA: The Alban Institute, 2010). (See page 64.)

Closing Prayer

Offer the following prayer, which is part of the prayer given by the author at the end of the chapter 5:

Gracious and holy God, pour out your Holy Spirit that brings us hope even in the midst of exile. In Christ, you proved that you want our welfare, not our harm. In Christ, you showed that forgiveness comes on the other side of judgment, and that you are giving us a future with hope. This day we commit ourselves to you; in the name of Jesus Christ our Lord. Amen.

Litany

All: **Hopelessness shrinks the radius of possibility.**

Group 1:   Hopelessness becomes apathetic;

Group 2:   Entraps;

Group 1:   Minimizes options;

Group 2:   Resigns to existing conditions;

Group 1:   Hopelessness loses heart.

All: **Hopefulness remembers the future so we will not remain trapped in the present arrangement of things.**

Group 2:   Hopefulness stirs imagination;

Group 1:   Expands horizons;

Group 2:   Influences events;

Group 1:   Energizes;

Group 2:   Creates a sense of buoyancy.

All: **I know the plans I have in mind for you, declares the LORD; they are plans for peace, not disaster, to give you a future filled with hope. When you call me and come and pray to me, I will listen to you. When you search for me, yes, search for me with all your heart, you will find me (Jeremiah 29:11).**

CPSIA information can be obtained
at www.ICGtesting.com
Printed in the USA
LVHW01s2131090817
544440LV00002B/3/P